BUILD-A-BOOK:
A PREWRITING PROCESS

THE KEY TO WRITING A BETTER BOOK FASTER

ERIKA KELLY

*This book is dedicated to the many
patient, insightful teachers I've had along the way.*

INTRODUCTION

Many years ago, a friend and I were hiking in the Santa Monica mountains, when we came upon a strange sight. I made up a story about what happened, involving aliens and soul-stealing, and she said, "You should be a writer."

Five simple words tilted the world in just the right way to make all my pieces finally fit together.

I'd never told anyone about the stories playing in my head. Why would anyone want to know about those scenes I made up to help me fall asleep each night?

That friend and I went home and started writing screen-plays together. And, let me tell you, they were fantastic—fresh and fun and wildly exciting. Hollywood *needed* them. And, so, I asked a producer to read them, certain he'd be blown away by our wit and riveting storytelling.

Would you like to know what he said after reading (and I use that term loosely) them?

"I…um…uh…I don't know…well…ahhhh."

That's verbatim, by the way.

It was mortifying. To this day, some thirty years later, I still cringe when I think about that awful phone call.

Rejection has its benefits, though. It led me to craft. From the moment I hung up the phone, I've dedicated myself to learning storytelling techniques. Over many decades, I've studied James Frey, Syd Field, Linda Seger, Blake Snyder, Donald Maass, Dwight Swain, Christopher Vogler, Debra Dixon, Jennifer Crusie, and Michael Hauge…just to name a few. 😊

I'd like to tell you how much easier writing's become for me, but I can't. No way around it, it's just plain hard. Frankly, there's nothing more intimidating than trying to transfer the beautiful reel that's unspooling in your head onto the blank page. So, to make it easier and more efficient, I developed a prewriting process.

And it's changed the world for me.

This process isn't about plotting. It's about developing story elements before starting the first draft. Essentially, I work out character details and major plot points, and then I mark them on a map to track the external goals and the character and relationship arcs.

The great thing about it—beyond taking the stress out of staring at a blank page—is that now, when I write myself into a dead-end or have no idea what scene to write next, I can look at what page I'm on and refer to my map to see where I am in the story. That'll tell me what plot point I should be driving to or where my hero needs to be along his arc.

Before we get started, I have to stress that I haven't invented anything here. Basically, I've distilled what I've learned over the years from workshops and craft books into this process.

Also, it has to be said, this process works for *me*. I don't know what works for you, but I hope something you read will resonate and make things easier.

And that's the point. Making writing easier.

CHAPTER 1

STORY IDEA

THE BEST MOTIVATION you have to get your fingers flying over the keyboard is your story idea. You need to be excited about it. If you're not excited about *writing* it, how's it going to hold the interest of readers who have a million other books to choose from?

And the propane for your motivation is conflict.

So, before I do anything else, I develop my story idea until it's crackling with conflict. Enough to fuel a three-hundred-page novel.

There are three levels to a story idea:

> 1. The first one is your concept—and if you write romance, that's the trope. Second-chance romance, secret baby, fake engagement. There's lots of potential in those concepts, but you need more than the promise of potential to write a story.

2. The next level is the *high* concept. The bookshelves are filled with those tropes, and in this extremely competitive marketplace, we have to make our books stand out. We have to come up with a hook so exciting that when the reader hears the blurb she one-click's it. Soccer mom demon hunter? Slam dunk.

3. The high concept idea will get you excited to write your book, but it's not a story. It doesn't have a character, a goal, a conflict, or a plot. So, the third step is to develop your high concept idea into a premise—it has all that good stuff.

I'll use the Reese Witherspoon movie *Sweet Home Alabama* to illustrate the three levels.

1. The concept of the movie is Return to Hometown. We've seen that a million times. The character's aunt dies and leaves her the B&B, the husband cheats and empties her bank account, forcing her to go back home and live with her parents.

It's interesting, but there's not enough conflict to keep you excited about writing it. And here's the thing. When you're staring at the blank page and nothing's happening? When you're uninspired and get up to go rooting through your cabinets for snacks? It's because you're not writing conflict. It's conflict that glues us to our chairs.

2. So then, let's look at *Sweet Home Alabama* as a high concept idea: a woman needs her ex's signature on the divorce papers before her fiancé finds out she's already married.

That's fresh and fun, and we're starting to get some sparks.

3. But it's not fleshed out enough to start writing, so we need to turn it into a premise: when her fabulous boyfriend proposes, a country girl who reinvented herself into a big city fashion designer has to return home and convince her ex to sign the divorce papers.

In that sentence, we've got a character—a country girl turned big city fashion designer. But what's most interesting is that she's reinvented herself. That's the part that gives off sparks—we just know it's going to cause all kinds of trouble.

The premise gives us:

1. A set-up: her fabulous boyfriend proposes. The *fabulous* part is important because if she's got a lousy boyfriend, there won't be much conflict in deciding which man she chooses.

2. A problem: she's already married.

3. An antagonist in the ex since she has to *convince* him to sign the papers.

4. And a goal: to *get* him to sign the papers.

That's a fun story to write, because it's fresh and filled with conflict.

CHAPTER 2

GOAL, MOTIVATION, AND CONFLICT

NOT LONG AGO, I had a conversation with a blogger about a book we'd both read where the hero died at the midpoint. At the funeral, the heroine meets a new guy and spends the entire second half of the book falling in love with him. My blogger friend loved the book, and when I pointed out that the second half had no conflict, she said, "Not all stories need conflict." Turns out, she thinks stories with goals and conflicts are formulaic.

Well, here's the thing. During the second half of that book, I enjoyed the author's voice. I smiled at the banter between the couple, but there were no highs and lows; there was nothing that made me *have* to turn the page. I could've put the book down to grab a soda and easily gotten distracted by something else. And, frankly, I didn't *feel* anything.

And, ultimately, isn't that why we read? For the emotional journey?

It isn't the words on the page or the ideas or even the characters that deliver the emotional experience. It's their timing in the story that does. The *structure*. Structure gives form to our words and ideas. It gives the story a rhythm, an escalation, and a catharsis for all the unbearably rising tension.

A character's goal engages the reader by giving her something to root for. It pulls her in by making her *have* to turn the page in order to find out what's going to happen. A character's motivation gets our readers emotionally invested. Her battle to achieve her goal—that escalation in urgency—is what makes their hearts pound. And it's the cathartic ending that makes them laugh, cry, or swoon.

These elements aren't formula. They're how we deliver meaning.

Let's look at each element individually. We'll start with goals.

CHAPTER 3

GOALS

EACH CHARACTER HAS TWO GOALS, an external one and an internal one. The external goal is the spine of your story. It's what your character's going to pursue from the first plot point until the climax, when she either wins or loses it.

If we want the reader to root for it, the goal needs to be specific. Something she can picture clearly in her mind. It should be so specific that every reader will have the *same* picture of what it will look like when your heroine wins her goal.

If your character wants to be rich, for example, I might envision her with a roomy apartment in a nice neighborhood and a car that doesn't break down. Someone else might imagine her winning the lottery and running out to buy a yacht. So, be sure the goal is clearly defined: she wants to get a promotion at work. Or she wants to sell ten acres of land to pay off her mortgage.

A goal needs two other attributes to get our readers invested in the character's pursuit. It should have high stakes and be urgent.

I'm going to use my book *Take Me Home Tonight* as an example. The heroine, Mimi Romano, just got her MBA with the expectation that her dad will hire her.

So that's her goal of the book: get her dad to hire her.

Mimi's goal is *specific*. She wants to be a restaurateur at her father's company.

The *stakes are high*. If her goal was just to get a job, we wouldn't care all that much about her dad hiring her. There are plenty of jobs out there for someone with an MBA. But this is a job her father's promised her since she was a little girl. She wants *this* job. Her entire identity is wrapped up in it, so if she doesn't achieve her goal, she doesn't know who she'll be.

And it's *urgent*: she's entered a six-week cooking competition. If she doesn't win, her dad won't hire her, and she'll be unemployed.

Now, the idea of wanting her dad to hire her doesn't sound like a wildly compelling story goal. Neither does getting your ex to sign the divorce papers. Those goals only become important when we understand the character's soul-deep reason for wanting to achieve them.

That job isn't just a paycheck for Mimi. It's her desperate need for her father's love. The universal need for unconditional love is what the reader taps into and roots for.

Which brings us to her internal goal. If the external goal is the spine of the story, the internal goal is the beating heart. Your character has a deep-seated wound or fear that holds her back from becoming who she's truly meant to be. She's not aware of it, but it's going to try to get her attention throughout the story until she can no longer ignore the call.

So, Mimi's external goal is to get her dad to hire her. That's a conscious pursuit. That's what she *wants*. She'll spend the entire book going after it.

Her internal goal is to feel worthy. It's a subconscious pursuit. It's what she *needs* to be a balanced, whole person. What she wants is in conflict with what she needs.

Both of these goals need to be tied together. And the way you do that is to make the external goal the physical representation of the internal goal. Internally, Mimi needs to feel worthy, so I make that visible by giving her the external goal of getting her dad to hire her. If he does, it'll mean he wants to spend time with her—something her workaholic dad has rarely done. It will prove she's worthy of love.

Your story is really about the internal goal. We just externalize it so the reader can see it, feel it, and experience it.

Motivation

You've got one specific goal your character is going to pursue all the way through to the climax, and now you need to develop her reasons for wanting it.

Truly, the fun part is coming up with the motivation because it turns your character into a three-dimensional human being. I never fill out character work sheets. I don't care about his favorite color or food, what kind of car he drives, or whether he wears boxers or briefs. All of that comes out organically as I'm writing. I care about what's holding him back from living his authentic life. I care about his fears and, most importantly, what he wants versus what he needs.

For this section, I rely on Michael Hauge's Inner Journey, so I'll briefly run through my take on the questions with you.

1. **What does your character need?** This is the internal goal we were just talking about. It's the subconscious need she'll eventually have to fulfill in order to become whole and balanced. Mimi *thinks* working with her dad will bring her happiness, but we know it doesn't work like that. The truth is that she needs to stop looking to her father to find her self-worth. What she *needs* is to find her own happiness. To feel worthy on her own. Mimi *wants* to work with her dad, but she *needs* to find her own path. This conflict between what she wants versus what she needs is the tension fueling the story.

2. **What is your character's longing?** She's not self-aware enough to know what she truly needs at the start of your story, but she does yearn for something. Something's missing in her life, but

she's just not willing to go through the kind of upheaval necessary to get it. While Mimi's applying for jobs and trying to get her dad to hire her, she's taken a temporary job cooking for a local rock band. She's not a chef, so she's just making basic food like spaghetti and roasted chicken, but what she really enjoys is baking. She's always got something in the oven for the guys. She'd never consider being a baker, though, because what kind of career is that for a driven, ambitious woman? So, how do we get Mimi to realize what she should be doing? We give her the embodiment of her longing. We give her cooking lessons with the hero, Calix Bourbon, and his fun and free-spirited family. It's what sparks the fire in her. Of course, she can't become a baker, though, until she completes her character arc.

3. **What is your character's wound?** Something happened to your protagonist before the story began. She went through an ugly divorce, her mom died when she was six, her father was an alcoholic. Whatever it was, that experience shaped her perception about how the world works. For Mimi, an entire childhood of her dad not spending time with her made her feel she wasn't worthy of his love.

4. **What is your character's false belief?** That wound created a fear. If her own dad can't love her, then she must not be worthy of *anyone's* love. Now, that's obviously a false belief. Her father has his own issues, and she can't paint everyone with

the same brush. But it *is* a logical conclusion for a child to make. Of course, her dad isn't one-dimensional. *Every* character in your story has a motivation. Mimi's dad moved from Italy to Brooklyn when he was a little boy. His father was a tailor, and they never had enough money to pay for rent, food, and clothes. So, *his* false belief is that if he slows down, he could wind up hungry and homeless again. And, ironically, he loves his daughter so much that he can't risk having her experience that kind of insecurity. That's his hot button. He wants the people he loves to be safe.

5. **What is your character's persona?** To protect herself from the terrible pain of believing she's unlovable, she's created a persona, a mask that she shows the world. Mimi presents herself as a brash, tough businesswoman. The kind of woman she thinks her dad would want to hang around.

6. **What is your character's authentic self?** If she'd never been hurt by her dad, if her spirit were still intact, who would she be? Mimi would be a baker. The best memories from her childhood come from baking desserts with her grandma and her dad. She's got a real talent and passion for it. That's her authentic self.

We read books for the emotional journey. The vehicle for that journey is your relatable, empathetic character. And motivation is the way to make your reader care about what happens to her.

CHAPTER 4

CONFLICT

CONFLICT IS SIMPLE. Your character has a goal, and his antagonist blocks it.

Two dogs, one bone.

There are multiple sources of conflict: man vs self, man vs society, man vs nature, etc. But I write romance, and I'm going for the emotional jugular, so I work with man against man. A protagonist versus an antagonist.

And, since fiction's about the emotional journey, the more personal we make the conflict, the more it's going to hurt your protagonist. The fact that Mimi's *father* is her antagonist is devastating. If the person blocking her were just another candidate competing for the same job, it wouldn't have the same emotional punch.

The person who means the most to her in the world blocks her from getting what she wants.

I consider three different elements of conflict. The first is the overarching conflict of the book. I think about it in two ways for the hero, the heroine, and the antagonist:

1. Who's blocking the external goal? Mimi wants her dad to hire her, but he blocks her from the moment she announces she's doing the cooking competition at the first plot point until the climax, where she finally presents an idea so worthy he has to hire her.
2. Who's blocking her internal goal? Mimi needs to feel worthy of her dad's love, but every time they have plans he's either on his phone or exhausted from difficult meetings and can't see her. That blocks her goal of feeling worthy.

The antagonist is Mimi's dad. His external goal is to get his daughter job experience in Florida. He believes if he hires her now, his team will think she got the job out of nepotism. They won't respect her. Mimi blocks his goal by refusing to leave Manhattan and entering a cooking competition instead. His *internal* goal is to feel safe. Mimi blocks that goal by refusing to do what he knows is the right way to build her career. She's going to fail, and he's not going to be able to stand seeing the daughter he adores unemployable.

Conflict is on every page of your book. In each scene, the point of view character has a goal and someone's blocking it. But the story goal—the one that isn't resolved until the climax, doesn't begin until the first plot point, a quarter of the way into the book.

So, what kind of conflict happens in the first quarter of the book? You've got a character committed to the status quo, who gets a call to action. People resist change, which means this incident has to be personal. Remember *Romancing the Stone*? Joan Wilder would never have embarked on an adventure if her sister hadn't called to say she'd been kidnapped. Your story doesn't need that much drama; the call just needs to be compelling to your character.

In the opening scene of *Take Me Home Tonight*, Mimi's waiting for her dad to finish a business meeting so they can hang out together. When he finally calls, it's to say he's too tired, and he'll see her another time.

Simple conflict, right? Mimi wants to see her dad but can't, because her dad's exhausted and wants to get back to the city. That doesn't seem like much of a wake-up call. But we're building momentum. Each scene pushes her a little harder, forcing her to move out of complacency. So, when her dad tells her he's got a job for her in Florida, that's the final straw.

At the first plot point, a quarter of the way into the book, Mimi decides to stop waiting for her dad to hire her and enters a cooking competition.

From that moment on, all the way to the climax, she's going after her story goal, and the antagonist is blocking every attempt.

It's in the climax—at almost ninety percent into the book —that the story conflict is resolved. Either the protagonist wins—Mimi's Dad hires her—or the antagonist does— Mimi takes the job in Florida.

I've got two other elements of conflict I consider. Let's dig into the next one.

CHAPTER 5

CRUCIBLE

IN SCIENCE, a crucible is a bowl in which chemicals are heated to very high temperatures. This causes them to change in the process. In fiction, it's when the conflict heats up so high the characters are forced to change. In other words, their tried and true ways of coping won't work in this new situation, so unless they try something new they won't achieve their goal.

The conflict forces them to change.

The key to the crucible in fiction is that the character can't get out of her dilemma in any way other than solving it. If your heroine can walk away from the conflict, then the stakes aren't high enough.

So, there's a crucible in the external conflict. For Mimi and her dad, the crucible is the job. Mimi must get hired by her dad. She's spent six years in college and graduate school with the sole intent of becoming a restaurateur like her father. Every summer she's taken internships in the field. She is a restaurateur. If he doesn't hire her, who will she be? It will be the death of her identity.

But Mimi's dad can't give her the job right now, because it'll hurt her career, and she'll wind up unsafe. That's unthinkable to him. So, they're locked in that conflict over the job. Neither can walk away from it.

There's also the crucible in the romance. For Mimi and her love interest, Calix, the crucible is the cooking lessons. Calix's family suffered a terrible loss, and his mom hasn't been coping well. He believes the lessons will draw her out of her cave. And it's working. For the first time in three years, she's back with her family. She's happy. So, no matter what's going on between him and Mimi, there's not a chance he's going to walk away from the lessons.

Mimi can't walk away from the lessons because, without them, she'll lose the cooking competition.

The crucible intensifies the relationship. Times are going to get tough for your couple. Every beat of your story brings them closer to their authentic selves, and that's terrifying. They don't ever want to feel the pain of their wounds again. At some point, they'll want to bail out of the conflict and run from the relationship, but you've got the crucible to force them to stay together and *build* their relationship.

Other examples of the romance crucible? If your hero gets his one-night stand pregnant, the baby's the crucible. If your heroine's mom marries the hero's dad, the familial relationship is the crucible. If they're stuck together in a cabin because of a snowstorm, the weather's the crucible.

CHAPTER 6

ROMANCE CONFLICT

THE ROMANCE CONFLICT is the third level I consider —this, too, happens on an external and internal level.

1. The external conflict is something outside your couple's control that prevents them from being together.

- Their families hate each other.
- He's a priest.
- She's got amnesia and can't remember him.
- They're from different socio/economic/religious backgrounds.
- Their personalities: he's a stern stoic man, and she's a vibrant, effervescent woman.
- A secret.
- A lie.

These are the tried and true plot devices. For Mimi and Calix, he's a temporary keyboard player with a band; she's their temporary cook. That's your classic office romance trope, only set in the world of rock 'n roll.

For Mimi, if she falls in love with Calix—this slacker guy who doesn't commit to anything—it threatens her very identity. She's a driven businesswoman. That's who she needs to be in order to spend time with her dad. So, if she falls for some temporary keyboard player and starts hanging out with his punk rock family, her father won't want to hang out with her. There's a lot at stake for her if she allows her feelings for Calix to grow.

2. The internal conflict is the most powerful. It stems from the wound we've been talking about. For Calix, falling in love with Mimi means taking his eyes off his mom, and that could lead to unthinkable consequences. He couldn't live with that. He believes with absolute certainty that he can't be in a relationship. Not even with someone as awesome as Mimi. But, the closer they get, the more willing he is to find compromises. He can just date her, right? Dating leads to the kind of attraction he can't resist, so he allows himself to have a physical relationship with her as long as she knows it can't lead anywhere. He keeps compromising until the lines blur, and he falls too deeply —at which point the unthinkable will happen, and he'll face the consequence he expected: thanks to his negligence, his mom gets hurt. For Mimi, falling for a man like Calix is dangerous, because he has the potential to marginalize her just like her dad does. That would be intolerable for her. So, she'll make compromises, too. Because she's falling in love with him and hoping he'll come to love her

so much, he'll change. Each step toward love comes with high stakes—and that's what creates compelling conflict.

So, to get the most emotional punch out of your story, you need to pair your protagonists with partners who offer the greatest threat to their comfort zones. The ones who dig up and expose the wound.

Why? Because they can't be free of the wound until they root it out, and there's not going to be any character growth unless we force the characters to change. It would be far too painful for Mimi to risk being with a man who might marginalize her. She'd never do it…unless that man happens to be her soulmate, in which case she'll have no choice but to fight her demons to win the gift of true love.

There's one last thing I work out for the romance conflict. Since a story's about a character's transformation, I like to think of the conflict between them as evolving, too. To show that evolution, I come up with one reason per act why each character believes a relationship can't work.

I think of it from their perspectives: why do they believe they can't get involved? Now, while most people use a three-Act structure, I break my books into four units. But all that means is I divide Act II into two sections. It's just easier for me to work in smaller pieces. So that means I come up with four reasons why they believe they can't be together.

In Act I, when Mimi meets Calix, she thinks he's smoking hot. He's got long hair, tattoos, and rides a Harley. But she's totally in her persona at that point, so he's not her type. She's into businessmen in smart suits and big watches.

In Act II, she's gotten to know him. She sees past her initial judgment and finds herself attracted to him, but she'd never date him because he's a slacker. He's a temporary keyboard player with a band, and he hangs out with his aimless childhood friends. She's still pretty deep in her persona, so she'd never date a guy who wasn't ambitious and driven.

Then we hit the midpoint, where they've made some form of commitment to each other, so by Act III (or, if you use a three-Act structure, it's just the second half of Act II), they're involved in each other's lives. He's teaching her how to cook; she's getting to know his family. Mimi's falling for him, but Calix has made it clear he doesn't date. And she's not going to have a one-night stand with him. So that's her third excuse.

And then, in the final act, when she's fallen in love with him, he hurts her badly. So her fourth and final reason, the one that comes when she's her authentic self, is her realization that he's just like her dad. He'll never put her first. She'll always be jumping through hoops because his attention is elsewhere.

So, while the trope is a great starting point for why they can't be together, the closer they get, the more their internal conflicts will rise. Intimacy is scary. Being rejected when you're your authentic self is devastating.

The deeper you get into the book, the more their internal conflicts become the obstacles, because those will have a deeper, more emotional impact.

CHAPTER 7

KEY ROMANCE QUESTIONS

WHILE WE'RE TALKING about the four reasons they can't be together, I'll mention the key romance questions I look at before I start writing.

1. **What is keeping the hero and heroine apart?** Here's where I come up with the four reasons for each of them.
2. **Why is the heroine the only woman in the world for him?**
3. **Why is the hero the only man for her?** First and foremost, the answer is because, while everyone else is buying their personas, they see each other for who they really are—and like them best that way. But there are other ways you can show how they're right for each other. For example, if she's dealing with grief, maybe he's had some experience with it and can help shed some light on the grieving process. If she's a pessimist, maybe he's a dreamer, and they balance each

other out. Maybe they both share the same wound, and so they recognize it in each other. If so, it can help them sort out their issues. Whatever you choose, keep in mind that your hero and heroine get along great when they're their authentic selves but are at odds when they're in their personas.

CHAPTER 8

EMOTIONAL VALUES

NEXT UP IS the emotional value of your story. As we've already discussed, we don't deliver emotional stories because we're naturally brilliant storytellers. It's something we craft.

So, to make sure I deliver the best emotional experience possible, I figure out three emotional values before I start writing a book.

1. The first is for the overall story. How do you want your readers to feel when they close the book? Do you want them to be unsettled—like, *Wow, that was a close call. I wasn't sure they'd work it out.* Or shocked, like *What the heck just happened?* Do you want them to swoon? Do you want them to hug the book and wish it hadn't ended? I figure out what I want my reader to feel, write it on a Post-It, and stick it next to my screen. It'll ensure I drive the story toward that emotion.

2. The other two values are for each of the protagonists. What's the driving emotion of your hero and heroine through the book? To figure that out, I look at their motivation. In *Take Me Home Tonight*, Calix lost his youngest brother three years before the story starts. It just about destroyed the family, but his parents encouraged the remaining kids to carry on with their lives. Calix was about to go on tour with his band when a sixth sense drove him home to check in with his mom. He entered a still, quiet house, and the hairs on the back of his neck went up. When he got to his mom's bedroom, he found she'd overdosed. He's lived with that image for the last three years, and he's waiting for her to do it again. Fear drives him through this story. It informs every decision he makes. Every time he takes a step closer to the heroine, fear grabs hold of him and reminds him he can't be distracted by relationships right now. He can't take his eyes off his mom.

3. Mimi wants to work with her dad. He told her if she went to an Ivy League university, he'd hire her, but he didn't. He told her she needed to get her MBA and *then* he'd hire her. Once again, he didn't. Now, at the start of the book, he throws out one more hoop: if you get work experience, I'll hire you. Mimi's had enough of his hoops. So, when she scores a spot on a nationally televised cooking competition, she takes it, determined to get the job on her own terms. What drives her

through the story is determination. It infuses her
every thought and action.

I don't start writing until I know how I want the reader to
feel when she closes the book and what emotions drive my
two main characters through it.

CHAPTER 9

ANTAGONIST

THE ANTAGONIST GETS his own section because he's just as important as the protagonist.

You don't have a story without him. Your conflict starts when he steps onto the page and ends when either he or the protagonist wins. So, I go through the same goal, motivation, and conflict with him as I do for my hero and heroine.

I give him a specific goal and a reason for wanting it. I make it personal. And I make it in direct opposition to the hero's goal.

A couple of things about the antagonist:

1. At the start of your story, he's more powerful than your hero. Why? Because at that point your hero's fully in his persona. He's clueless about his wound, and he's living with a false belief of the world. That means he has no skills to help him

on this journey he's about to take. Your antagonist, though, is fully prepared, which is what makes him more powerful. It's the antagonist's first move that knocks the hero out of his comfort zone and forces him to take the first step into the story. And it's his competence that forces the hero to wake up, shake off his complacency, and actually engage in his life.

2. Try to find ways in which the antagonist and protagonist are alike. It'll make your character's journey even more powerful and emotional if your hero sees himself in the antagonist—if he's one bad decision away from *becoming* the antagonist. It's just another layer of tension in the story.

CHAPTER 10

CHARACTER ARCS

NOW THAT I'VE got the basic elements worked out, I map out the character arc.

Again, I'm not a plotter. I don't figure out every scene in the book, but I start placing markers along a plot map to make sure the transformation develops at a believable pace.

The character arc goes one hundred eighty degrees from one pole to another, from one state of being to the opposite state. So, the first thing I do is get an aerial view of it. Is she going from isolation to integration? Self-doubt to self-confidence? Fear to courage?

Mimi starts out relying on her father for her sense of worth and ends up self-reliant. Calix goes from Fear to Trust. We've got three hundred pages to enact that huge, dramatic change. And we can't have any big jumps. It has to be believable.

In the opening scene, the character's at the start of her arc. Mimi's waited all weekend in the Hamptons for her dad to find time to spend with her before he heads back to the city. When he finally gets in touch, it's to say he's tired and he'll see her another time. She can't believe her dad couldn't find a minute to spare for her. In Calix's first scene, he's checking on his mom. Making sure she joins the family for a meal. Both of them are living completely in their personas.

Mimi gets her dad to agree to a drink. Her first step towards transformation comes when he tells her he's found a great opportunity for her in Florida. Now, if he'd said he had a great job for her in New York, she might've taken it. But he said Florida. And what's her issue? She wants her dad to spend time with her. That's how she'll know she's worthy. So, when he offers to send her to Florida, he's just flat-out told her he doesn't want her around. *Ouch*.

That major blow, which is the inciting incident, forces her to step out of her comfort zone—which was following her dad's advice. She takes her first step in moving away from him by flagging down the motorcycle that's driving down the street and asking for a ride. Hello, hot, inked Calix Bourbon. He's as opposite from her dad as you can possibly get.

The next step she takes is joining the cooking competition. She's completely out of her element there because she's a businesswoman with an MBA. She's not a professional chef, so she's got to learn quickly. Calix, a guy who's not her type at all and whose parents are former punk rockers, offers to help her. So, all through the book, we keep pushing her, forcing her to change. As Calix and Mimi work together, he keeps pointing out how weird it is that she insists on working with her dad when there are so many other opportunities out there, just as she points out to him how futile his efforts are in influencing his mom's state of mind. Each one pushes the other to see the truth. To live an authentic life.

The key to making your character arc believable is to take your time. Don't rush the transformation. The bottom line is people don't want to change. Maybe life isn't great, but if they change the status quo, they might wind up with something worse. So, we have to force our characters to step out of their comfort zones. And, to do that, we make it personal. Mimi would never have taken that first step if her dad hadn't tried to send her to another state. *That* motivated her to take action.

It's simple to track the changes in the character arc because they turn on the key plot points. I write them in alongside the external turning points to make sure there aren't any big leaps in growth.

Opening scene: your protagonist is fully in her persona. Mimi's waiting for her dad to find time to hang out with her.

Inciting incident: your antagonist does something that forces your hero out of his comfort zone. He must embark on this journey. For Mimi, she flags down Calix and takes off on his Harley, leaving her dad standing on the sidewalk, shocked and horrified.

Plot point 1: what happens here must be such a big deal that your character is forced to try something she's never done before. Her old coping skills won't work so, once she crosses that boundary by trying something new, she changes. Deeply upset that her dad wants her to move to another state, Mimi enters the cooking contest.

Midpoint: whatever your protagonist does here, it burns the bridge between who she was at the start of the story and who she's become. She can't go back to her persona.

Mimi and Calix make love. Spending time with his punk rock family takes her away from her father's world. In terms of her arc, she's stepping out from behind her persona and becoming her authentic self.

Crisis: your protagonist faces her deepest fear. For Mimi that would be opening her heart to someone and having him marginalize her just like her dad does. And that's exactly what Calix does. His family faces a crisis that threatens his mom's well-being—*his* greatest fear—and he pushes Mimi aside so he can take care of it. Their deepest fears collide, and both go running back into their personas. But, of course, they don't fit anymore. So they've got no choice but to keep fighting.

Climax: now that she finally has all the skills she needs, Mimi wins the battle against her father. He hires her.

Resolution: But, since she's finally become her authentic self, she no longer wants the job. She's going to own a tea shop with her rocker friends.

CHAPTER 11

PLOT MAP

ONCE I'VE WORKED out all the details, I make the plot map. On it, I mark all the major turning points, so that I can keep track of the development of the external goal and the relationship and internal arcs. This isn't about knowing what scenes I'm going to write. It's about pinning structural landmarks on my map to keep me from veering off the road.

It's about giving me an aerial view of my story, so that when I have no idea what scene to write next I can look at the map and see where I am and what plot point I should be driving to.

As I said earlier, I like to work in smaller units, so I use a four-act structure instead of three. It's just easier for me to drive my character through smaller bits of real estate than to contemplate the entire journey at once.

First, let's break down the acts so we understand the action in each one.

In Act I we set up the story world. We introduce the heroine, show what's missing in her life, reveal the cast of characters, and formulate the overarching story questions of the book. In a romance, the question is always will Mimi and Calix get together. Additionally, the hero and heroine have their own story questions. Will Mimi get her dad to hire her? Will Calix free himself from the responsibility of his mom's well-being?

In Act II, the character sets off to achieve her goal. This section is about reacting. The antagonist throws up obstacles, and the heroine reacts to them. Everything is new to her, and she doesn't have the skills to navigate this new world just yet.

In Act III, after the midpoint, your character is fully committed to achieving her goal. Instead of reacting, she's now taking action against the antagonist, who's going after her with everything he's got. It ends in utter failure at the crisis.

In Act IV, our character gives up and retreats to her ordinary world to lick her wounds. But she's changed, so it no longer fits. She has an epiphany that frees her from her wound and, in her rebirth, she goes after her goal with everything she has and claims it. In the last few pages, we give a snapshot of the new world she's created.

This is what my final plot map looks like. For simplicity, I'm basing page numbers on a three- hundred-page book:

Act I: SET UP, p. 1 - 75

1. Opening scenes for both the hero and heroine, showing them in their ordinary worlds

2. Inciting Incident, p. 30:

- This is the moment things go sideways. It's when Mimi's dad tells her about the job in Florida.

3. The New Situation, p. 30 – 75.

- Here, our protagonists adjust to their new worlds. Mimi meets Calix's family and friends. They show her a whole other way to live, and that's meaningful because she's only ever been immersed in her father's world. She's still in her persona, so this world is not for her, no matter how intriguing. This is her glimpse into the kind of life she could have if she had the courage to be her authentic self.
- Here I give the first reason why my couple thinks they can't be together.

4. Act I ends with the first plot point on P. 75.

- This is the moment when everything changes. Your protagonist formulates a goal and goes after it.
- I also put the first kiss here to launch the romantic relationship.

Act II: REACT, p. 75 - 150

5.

- I start with an Aftermath scene. Your character's just had her world rocked by the first plot point, so she's going to need to react to what happened. She'll regroup and formulate a plan.
- There's also a Kiss Aftermath scene to show her reaction to the first brush with intimacy. Here's where I reveal the second reason why they can't be together.

6.

- Halfway through Act II I put in a Pinch Point. It's a reminder that the antagonist is out there. It doesn't have to be a big deal. It's just that, in the midst of learning how to cook and kissing and finding her way in this new world, Mimi needs a reminder of what's at stake. She could, for example, find out her dad's interviewing another candidate for the job.

7.

- There's also a romance pinch point, which is a complication for the romance. They're working together and liking each other more than they want to. So, we give them a reminder of why love is unsafe. For Calix, love is unsafe because he can't take his eyes off his family. So, right when he's enjoying Mimi, something happens with his mom that reminds him why he can't be in a relationship right now.

8. The Midpoint, p. 150

- There are two things to think about with turning points. One, they should be something the hero's never experienced before. And, two, it's good to think of them in terms of reversals. A roller coaster wouldn't be much fun if all it did was rise to the top and then plummet. Same with story. We want the reader to experience all kinds of emotions, so we shake things up. Since your protagonist loses everything in the Crisis, then the Midpoint should be some kind a victory.
- In a romance this means that, since the relationship's going to end at the Crisis, then at the midpoint the couple should make some kind of commitment. For me, this is where I put the first love scene.
- The midpoint is the point of no return. Your characters are now fully committed to the goal. From this moment on they're determined.

Act III: Determined Action, p. 150 – 225

9.

- At this point, your character's had enough of the antagonist's behavior, and she's done reacting. She's now taking action.

- So here, again, I start with an Aftermath scene, where they react to the midpoint. They're regrouping and formulating a new plan.
- On the romance arc, they're reacting to the commitment they just made—either freaking out or celebrating.
- Halfway through the third act, I put in a second pinch point. It's another reminder of the antagonist's power. This one should jerk the rug out from under them.
- There's also a second romance pinch point. They're now relating to each other mostly as their authentic selves, so that's scary. Here, for example, an ex could show up, reminding the heroine that the hero has loved someone else before and could go back to her.

Crisis, p. 225

- This is the moment they both face their deepest fears. Calix's family has suffered another blow—so big that his mom crawls back into her cave. He *knew* he shouldn't have gotten involved with Mimi. It wasn't the right time, and now look what happened. His greatest fear is realized—his mom's not talking to anyone. For Mimi, being shut out by Calix is *her* greatest fear. She's not worthy of being included in his life. She's marginalized, just like with her dad.
- On the external level, she's lost the cooking

competition, which means her dad won't
hire her.

Act IV: Resolution, p. 225 to the end.

10.

- We start with another aftermath scene. They've
  both just lost everything, so they're going to slink
  back into the comfort of their personas. Having
  faced their worst fears, they've decided love is
  NOT worth it, and now they're going to lick
  their wounds. This doesn't have to mean they
  wallow in self-pity and get drunk. You have to
  figure out how *your* character reacts to loss. For
  Mimi, she wants comfort food, so she takes her
  dad to the bakery she passes every day on her way
  to work. That's when a brilliant business idea
  forms, and she shares it with him. He hires her
  on the spot.

- They can't stay in their personas long. It's like
  wearing your jeans from high school—they no
  longer fit (well, mine don't). For Mimi, she's
  gotten what she wanted. Her dad finally hired
  her. But she's changed, and the job doesn't fit her
  anymore. So, she has an epiphany. Seeing what
  caused her wound allows her to shed her false
  belief. She's completely free. Calix has a
  conversation with his mom where he confesses
  his fears. She promises to do better and get the
  help she needs.

- The Climax comes about ninety percent into the story. Now that they're free and living fully as their authentic selves, they have all the skills they need to take down the antagonist. They formulate a new plan, a great plan, and they defeat the antagonist and win the greatest gift of all: true love.
- In a romance, I like to have a Grand Romantic Gesture. It can't be easy for Calix to win Mimi back after cutting her out of his life at the crisis. He needs to sweep her off her feet and, most importantly, prove to her that he's completely, irrevocably changed.
- Resolution: after all the drama, our readers want a moment to savor the victory. The couple they've been rooting for is now together. So, we give them a snapshot of the new world. We give them proof that our protagonists have really changed, and that's what convinces the reader that the couple will live happily ever after.

Erika Kelly's BUILD-A-BOOK Map

Act I	Act II	Act III	Act IV
SET-UP *p. 1-75*	**REACTING** *p. 75-150*	**DETERMINED ACTION** *p. 150-225*	**RESOLUTION** *p. 225-300*
• Opening scenes for hero and heroine: relatable, empathetic characters • Fully in identity/false belief • Reason #1 why h/h can't be together • Inciting Incident p. 30: first step into the story and out of their personas • New Situation p. 30-75: adjust to new world • Plot Point I: P. 75: story goal formed; first kiss.	• Aftermath scene: react/regroup • Reacting to antagonist • Step into authentic self/move away from false belief • 2nd reason why h/h can't be together • Pinch point I p. 110: reminder of antagonist • Romantic pinch point I; reminder that the relationship might not work • Midpoint p. 150; point of no return; make love	• Aftermath scene to midpoint and to making love: react/regroup • Move into essence/away from false belief • 3rd reason why h/h can't be together • Stakes higher/pace faster • Pinch point II p. 200: antagonist jerks rug out from under them • Romantic pinch point II: reminder of the threat to their relationship • Crisis p. 225: all is lost	• Aftermath: run back into persona • 4th reason why h/h can't be together • Epiphany: see truth of their wound • Fully in essence/truth • Climax/Grand romantic gesture p. 290: free from wound; claim the prize of true love • Snapshot of new world: proof that they've changed.

CHAPTER 12

BUILD-A-BOOK WORKSHEETS

HERO:
What's his external goal:
What's blocking him from reaching it:
What's his external reason for needing it:
What's his internal motivation:
What's his longing, the one he pays lips service to:
What does he truly need (unaware of it; the hole):
What's his wound:
What's his fear:
What's his false belief:
What's his persona:
What's his essence:
What's his arc in this story:

HEROINE
What's her goal:
What's blocking her from reaching it:
What's her external reason for needing it:
What's her internal motivation:

What's her longing, the one she pays lip service to:
What does she truly need (unaware of it; the hole):
What's her wound:
What's her fear:
What's her false belief:
What's her persona:
What's her essence:
What's her arc in this story:

<u>Crucible:</u>
What forces them to be together:

<u>Why can't they be together</u>:
1. External:
2. Excuse:
3. Internal:

<u>Antagonist:</u>
What does he want:
Why does he want it:

<u>Act I Set-up p. 1-75 (both fully in their personas)</u>

<u>Ordinary Worlds p. 1-34</u>:
What's the hero's ordinary world:
What's missing in his life/his hole:
What's his inciting incident:
What's the heroine's ordinary world:
What's missing in her life/her hole:
What's her inciting incident:

Opportunity p. 34

What's the meet cute:

What's the inciting incident that launches the two of them on this journey:

New Situation p. 34-85

What are some things they need to adjust to:

What excuse do they give for why they can't be together:

What's the glimpse of the life he could have if he had the courage to go after it:

What's the glimpse of the life she could have if she had the courage to go after it:

Plot Point I p. 85

What's the book's story question:

His arc: what decision does he make that forces him to take his first step out of his persona:

Her arc: what decision does she make that forces her to take her first step out of her persona:

What's the choice they make that pushes the relationship arc:

What's the choice they make that launches them into this story:

Act II: Progress p. 85-170 (take their first step out of their personas)

What are some fun scenes that show them getting to know each other:

What are some fun scenes that show they've got a handle on this problem:

Pinch point p. 125
What's his reminder of what's at stake in the story (antagonist):

What's her reminder of what's at stake in the story (antagonist):

Romance pinch point (reminder why love is unsafe):

Midpoint p. 170
What's his mirror moment?

What's her mirror moment?

What decision does he make that burns the bridge to his ordinary world?

What decision does she make that burns the bridge to her ordinary world?

Act III Complications and Higher Stakes p. 170-255 (try living in their essences)
What are some scenes that will show they're both in their essences:

What are some scenes that will show the antagonist is getting closer/stronger:

What tests his commitment to living in his essence:

What tests her commitment to living in her essence:

Pinch Point II p. 210
What does the antagonist do to pull the rug out from under him?

What does the antagonist do to pull the rug out from under her?

What happens to remind them that love is unsafe?

Crisis p. 255

How do their deepest fears collide:

What does he lose:

What does she lose:

Act IV Resolution p. 255- 325 (living fully in essences)

What's the aftermath of the crisis for him:

What's the aftermath of the crisis for her:

Epiphany p. 275

What's his epiphany:

What's her epiphany:

Climax: p. 300

Grand Romantic Gesture

Epilogue

CHAPTER 13

TIMELINE

READY TO JUMP into the first draft? Hang on. One last thing you need to do.

Our number one goal as authors is to suck our readers into our worlds and keep them there. The quickest way to kick them out is to have them flicking back a few pages to see how much time has elapsed or whether you've gotten the timing wrong. Easy solution.

Create a timeline. Start with your opening scene and track every single one after it to make sure you've got it right. The timeline is critical. I guarantee your readers will notice if you make a mistake.

Try to make it as invisible as possible. Instead of writing, Three days later, see how you can seamlessly weave it into the exposition or dialogue. And try to do it as early in the scene as possible.

Okay, that's it. Now jump into your first draft with the confidence of having a compass and a map.

CHAPTER 14

FINAL THOUGHTS

IF YOU'RE A PANTSER, and those page numbers and percentages make you anxious, let me just say that, in spite of everything we've just gone over, I'm actually an intuitive writer. If you pick up any of my books, it's unlikely you'll find an inciting incident on page 30 or a midpoint on page 150.

The point of this map is to make the first draft easier and more efficient. It's to guide me through the first couple of revisions when I've gotten totally lost in the weeds and have no idea how to fix the mess I've made. The map reminds me where I need to be in the story and what I should be driving towards.

Once I've got a solid structure, I don't look at the map again. So, don't let those numbers make you nervous. They're just a guideline. The map is a rope to pull you through.

Thank you for reading this book. I hope something in my prewriting process makes the first draft easier for you.

Good luck with your writing!

Erika

ABOUT THE AUTHOR

Award-winning author Erika Kelly writes sexy and emotional small town romance. Married to the love of her life and raising four children, she lives in the southwest, drinks a lot of tea, and is always waiting for her cats to get off her keyboard.

https://www.erikakellybooks.com/

facebook.com/erikakelly

instagram.com/erikakellyauthor

tiktok.com/@small_town_romance_books

x.com/ErikaKellyBooks

amazon.com/Erika-Kelly/e/B00L0MLWUY

bookbub.com/authors/erika-kelly

pinterest.com/erikakellybooks